JULIA

Learns How to Protect Life Wisely

by

Carla D'Addesi

illustrated by

Wendy Potzgo

Julia Learns How to Protect Life Wisely
Written by Carla D'Addesi
Illustrated by Wendy Potzgo

ISBN-13: 978-0692478707
ISBN-10: 0692478701

Copyright 2015 by Carla D'Addesi

Published by Tre Belle Sorelle

All rights reserved.

Printed in the USA.

The author grants exclusive rights for printing or reproduction of the work in any format including digital. To use any portion of this book, you must first obtain permission in writing to the publisher.

www.carladaddesi.com

This book is dedicated to
my three gifts of life:
Vittoria, Isabella and Giulia
and my precious nieces:
Nevaeh and Makayla

"Let's play in our big backyard!" said Julia.
Julia's cousins, Nay-Nay and Kay-Kay, were over to play.
Julia ran outside with her sisters and cousins.
It was a warm Spring day.
Seeds were sprouting. Birds were chirping. Flowers were blooming.
Julia saw life everywhere.

"One, two, three..." counted Julia. Nay-Nay studied the seedlings. Red tomatoes, orange carrots and green peas were growing in the garden.

"Mom says that we are doing a great job of protecting our vegetables from the weeds," said Julia. Her mom taught her that the seedlings will grow vegetables someday. Julia remembered her mom's wise words, "God created all life and all life must be protected, no matter how small."

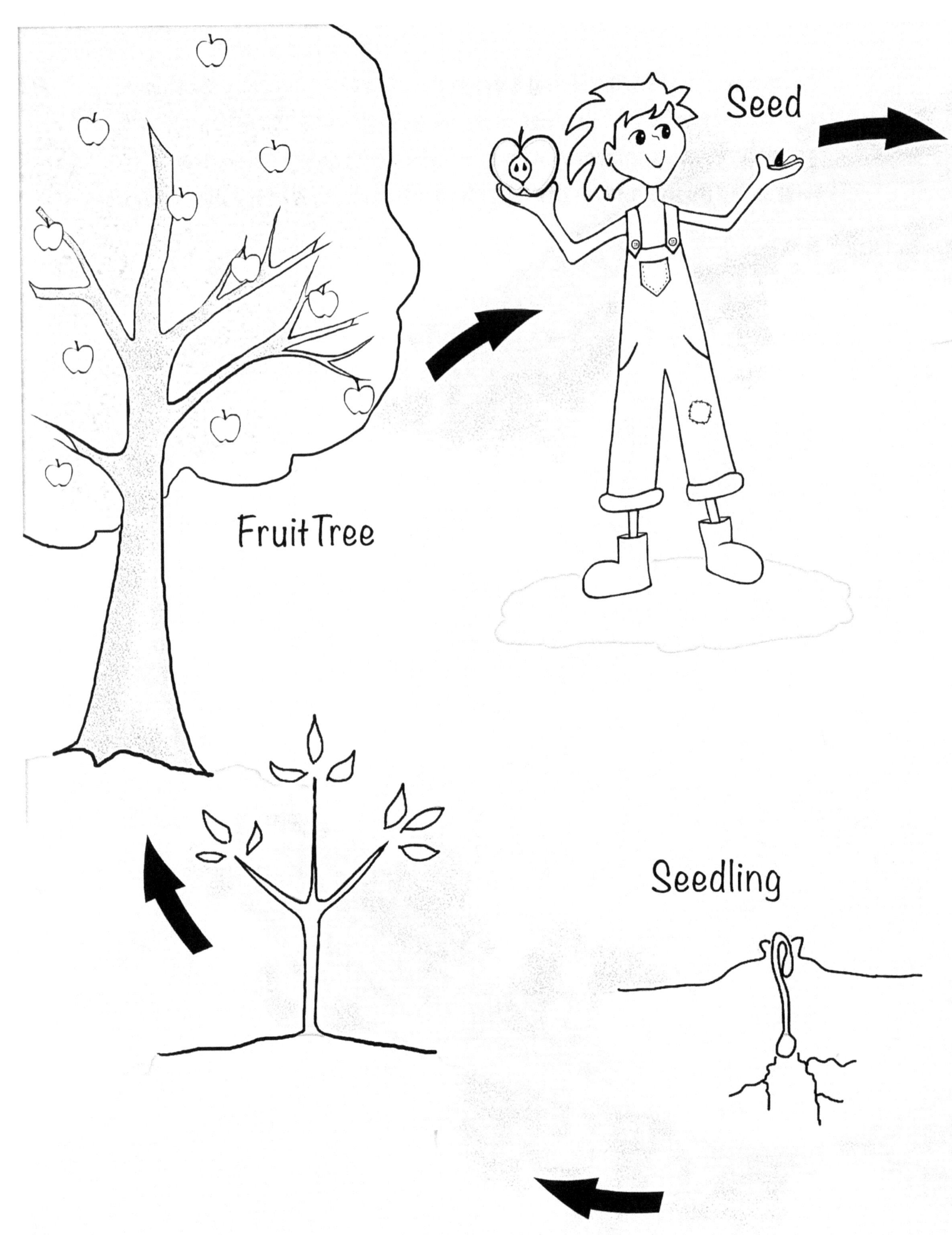

"We found a bird's nest!" said Julia's sisters.
They raced to the nest where they found tiny blue eggs.
She wondered what the baby bird looked like inside of the egg.
Did it have fluffy feathers? Was it a girl or a boy?
Her mom taught her that the baby birds were very tiny and would
be big birds someday.
Julia remembered her mom's wise words, "God created all life and all life must
be protected, no matter how small."

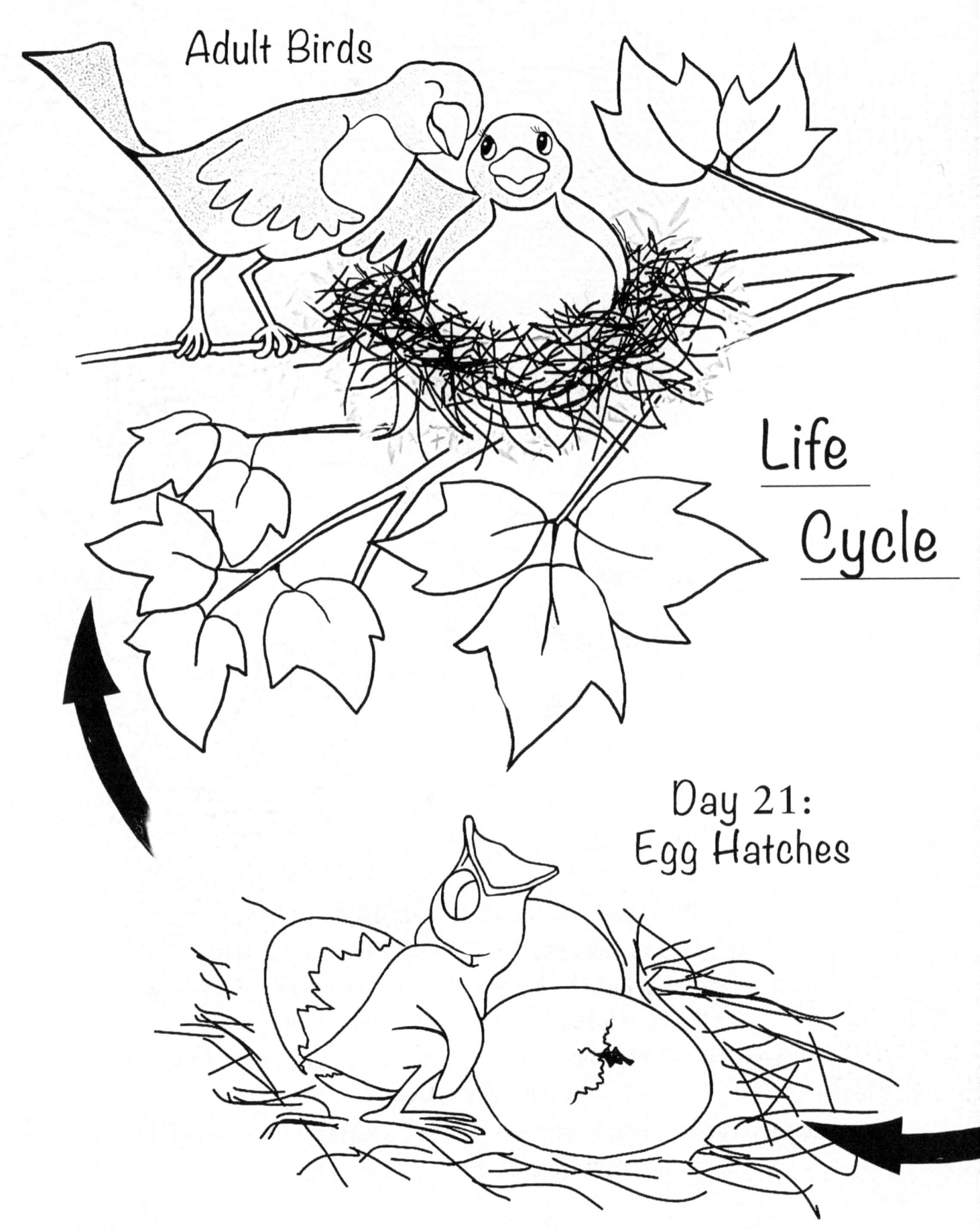

Life Cycle of a Bird

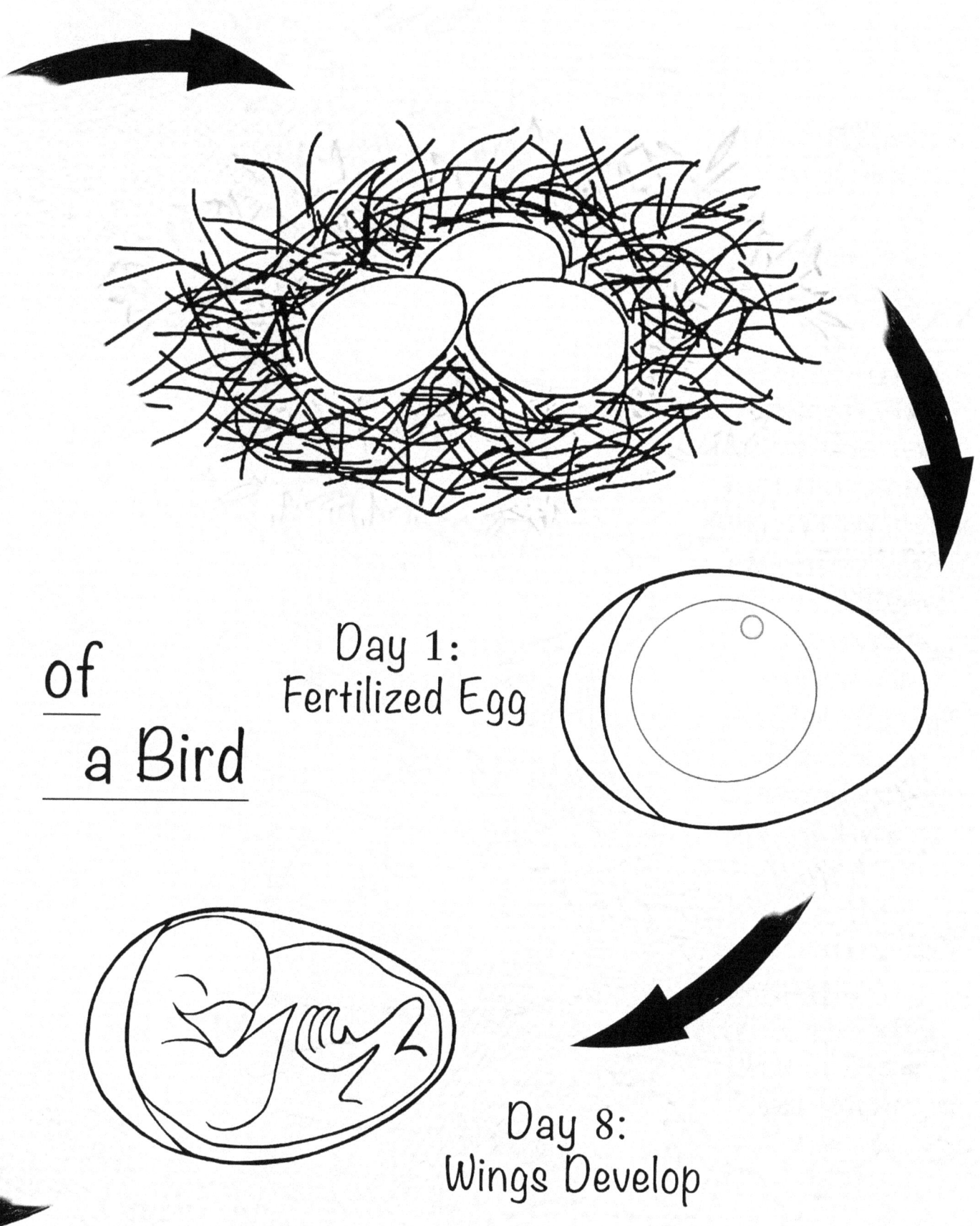

Day 1: Fertilized Egg

Day 8: Wings Develop

A caterpillar crawled on Julia's arm.

"Eww! Squash it!" said Kay-Kay.

Julia protected her fuzzy friend's life. Her mom taught her that this caterpillar was not yet a butterfly, but would become a beautiful butterfly someday. Julia wondered what the butterfly would look like. What color would it be? How high would it fly?

Julia remembered her mom's wise words, "God created all life and all life must be protected, no matter how small."

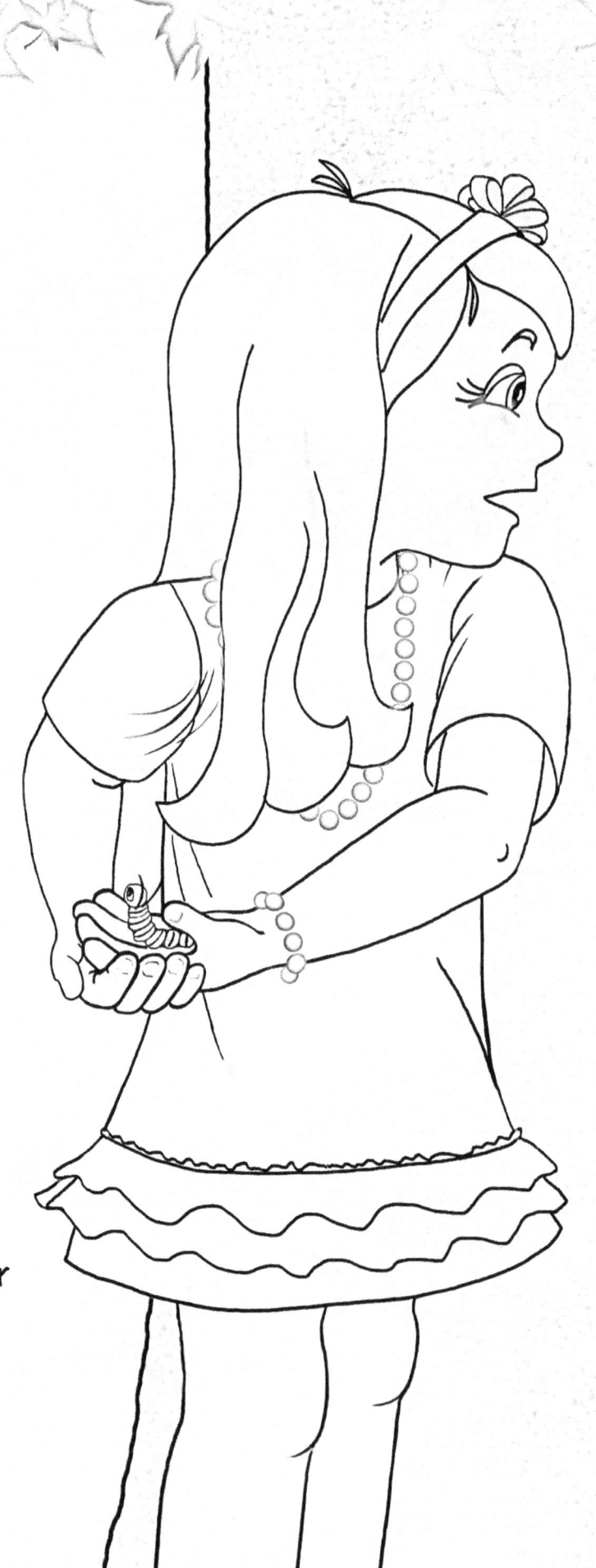

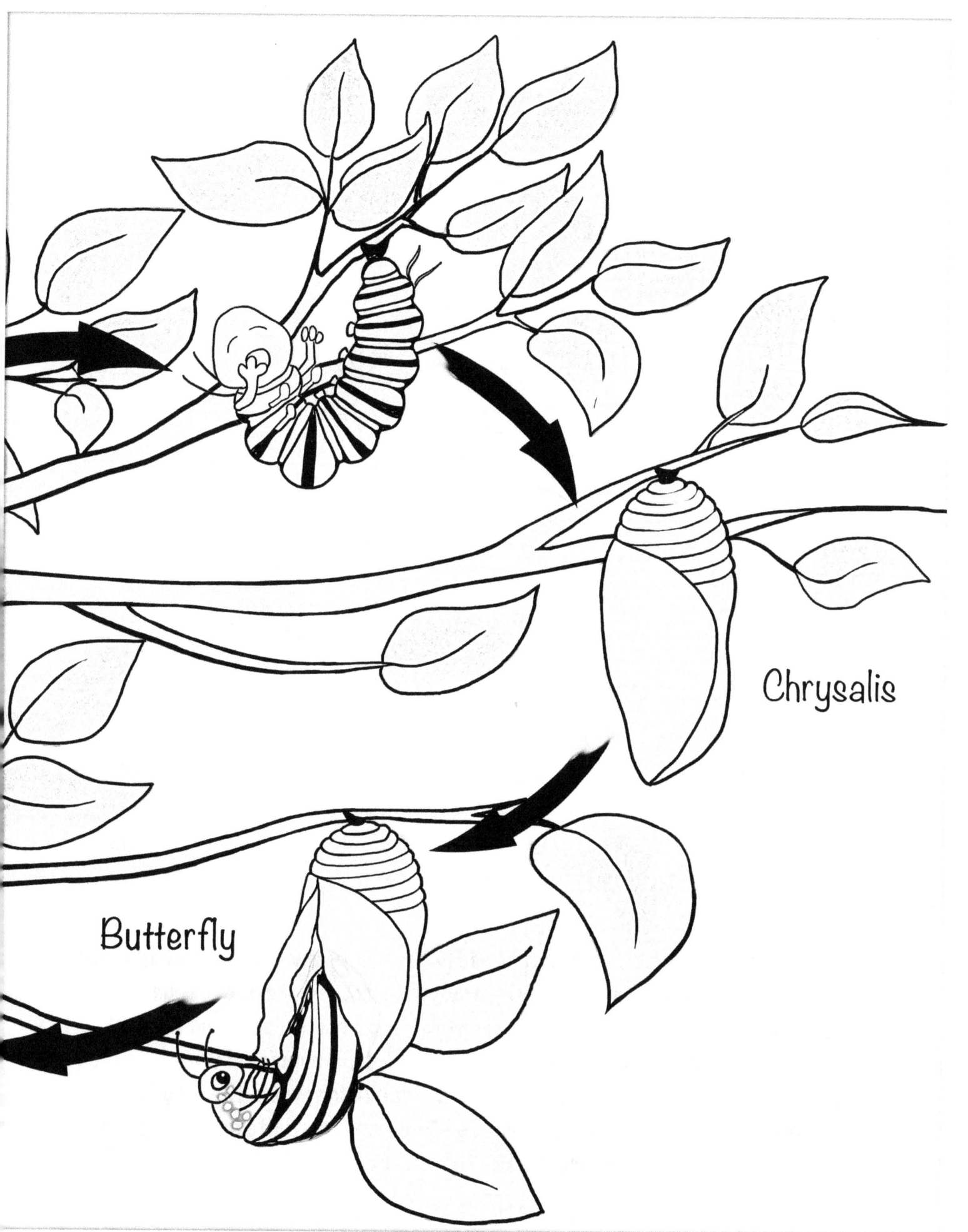

The caterpillar tickled Julia's hand and she let her fuzzy friend go near their stream. "Fish!" said Nay-Nay. "They are not fish. They are baby frogs called tadpoles," replied Julia. Her mom taught her that the tadpoles did not look like frogs yet, but would become frogs someday. Julia wondered what the frog would look like. How long would its legs be? How high would the frog jump? Julia remembered her mom's wise words, "God created all life and all life must be protected, no matter how small."

Life Cycle of a Frog

Adult Frog

Young Frogs

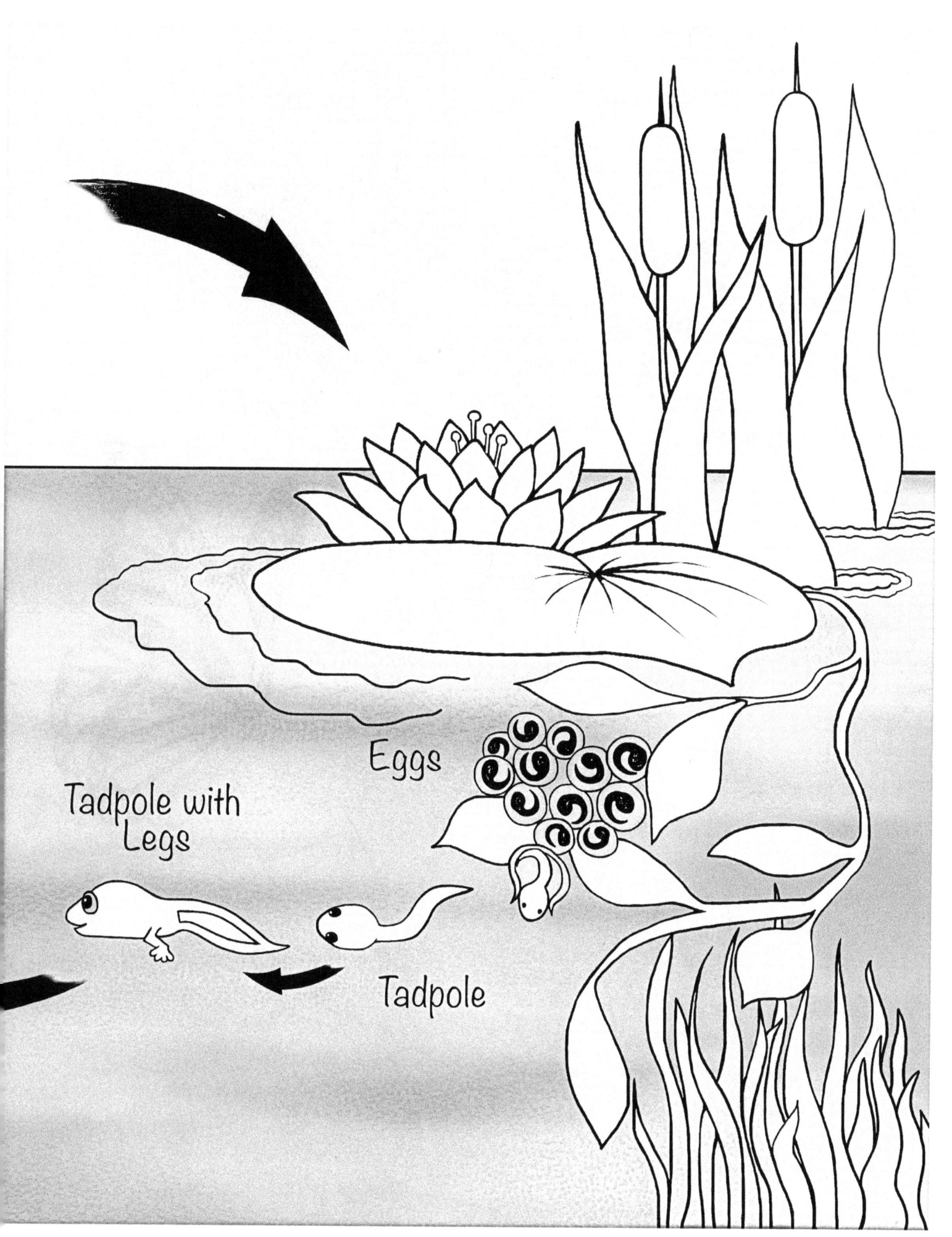

" Come to the garden!" called Julia's mom.
"Look! Mom made our favorite, butterfly sandwiches!" said Julia.
She loved eating in the flower garden.
She remembered when she helped her mom plant the little seeds and now they were big flowers.
Julia remembered her mom's wise words,
"God created all life and all life must be protected, no matter how small."

Seeds

Life Cycle of a Flower

Flower

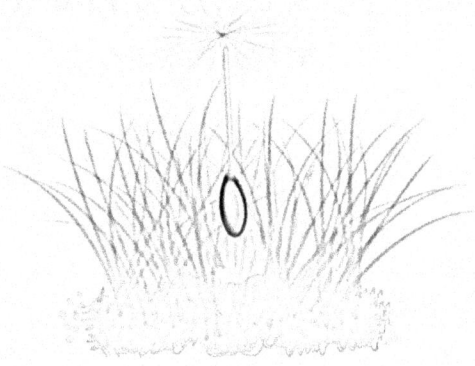

Seedling

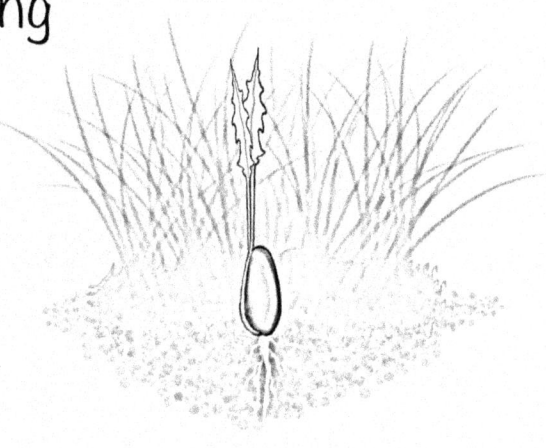

Julia looked at her cousins as they munched on their sandwiches. She loved their braided hair and brown skin. Julia's mom taught her that her cousins were adopted. "A mom who can't care for her baby will give her baby to a loving family to adopt." Julia was thankful that Nay-Nay and Kay-Kay's mom protected them while they were growing in her tummy.

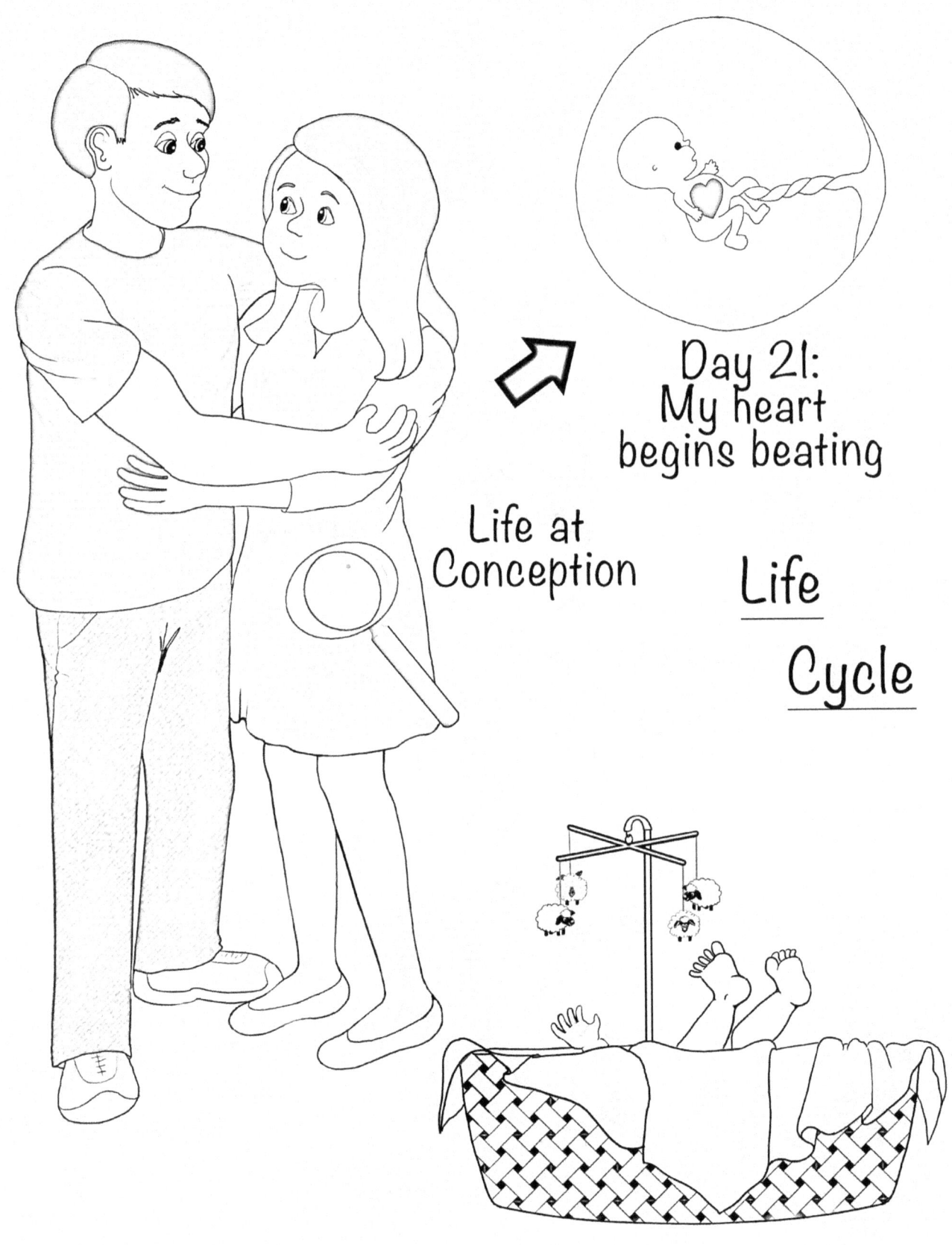

Week 13:
My very own fingerprints

Week 18:
I recognize my mommy's voice
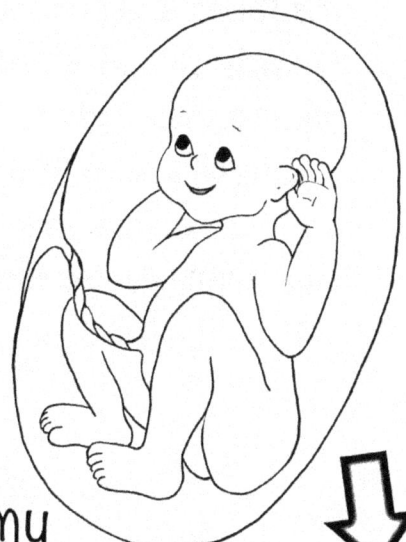

of a
BABY

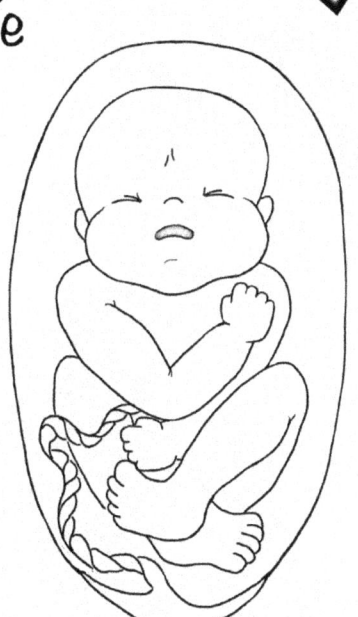
Week 20:
I feel pain, OUCH!

Week 40:
I'm ready to meet you Mom and Dad!
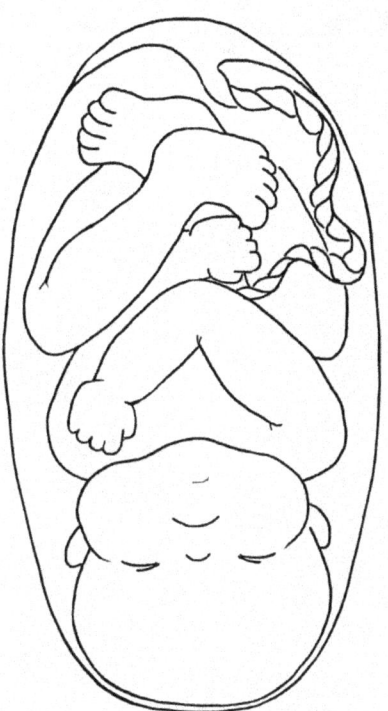

As the girls sat on their picnic blanket, Julia's mom said, "We must protect seeds, so that we can enjoy pretty flowers and yummy vegetables. We must protect eggs, so that we can enjoy the singing birds. We must protect caterpillars, so that we can chase butterflies. We must protect tadpoles, so that we can catch slippery frogs. We must especially protect babies in their mommy's tummies, so that we can enjoy lots of giggles, kisses and hugs!"

"Yes, God created all life! All life must be protected, no matter how small!" said Julia.

Other books by this Author!

Available at Amazon.com, barnesandnoble.com
and christianbookdistributor.com

 Wendy Potzgo is a world traveler but presently calls Pennsylvania home. She proudly supported her husband's travels abroad during his military service to our country. These travels to exotic places gave life to Wendy's illustrations. She studied art across the globe. She has produced countless greeting cards.

She is the exclusive illustrator for the "Julia Learns" series and enjoys using her God-given talents to champion for religious freedoms and liberties as reflected in her adorable drawings. Her greatest accomplishments are her two adult children and five grandchildren with whom she loves to spend time.

www.ingramcontent.com/pod-product-compliance
Lightning Source LLC
Chambersburg PA
CBHW081025040426
42444CB00014B/3359